PAINTING: 1945-1985

20th Century Art

PAINTING: 1945-1985

*By William S. Lieberman,
Lisa Mintz Messinger,
Sabine Rewald, and
Lowery S. Sims*

*Selections from
the Collection of
The Metropolitan
Museum of Art
New York*

Published by The Metropolitan Museum of Art, New York

John P. O'Neill, Editor in Chief
Barbara Burn, Project Supervisor
Teresa Egan, Managing Editor
Michael Shroyer, Designer

Library of Congress Cataloging-in-Publication Data

Metropolitan Museum of Art (New York, N.Y.)
  20th-century art.

  Includes index.
  Contents: v. 1. Painting, 1905–1945 / by William
S. Lieberman.—v. 2. Painting, 1945–1985 / by William S.
Lieberman, Lisa Mintz Messinger, Sabine Rewald, and Lowery S. Sims.
  1. Art, Modern—20th century. 2. Art—New York
(N.Y.) 3. The Metropolitan Museum of Art (New York, N.Y.)
I. Lieberman, William Slattery, 1924–   . II. Title.
N6487.N4M855 1987   709'.04'007401471   86-28430
ISBN 0-87099-484-0 (v. 1)
ISBN 0-87099-485-9 (v. 2)

Composition by The Graphic Word, New York
Printed and bound by Dai Nippon Printing Co., Ltd., Tokyo, Japan

Cover: Jackson Pollock: *Autumn Rhythm (Number 30),* 1950

INTRODUCTION

ON July 4, 1866, a group of Americans gathered in Paris to celebrate their national holiday and to propose for the City of New York a "National Institution and Gallery of Art." The proposal became a project, progress was rapid, and in 1870 The Metropolitan Museum of Art was created. Among its founders were three painters, Frederic E. Church, John F. Kensett, and Eastman Johnson; the architect Richard Morris Hunt, who in 1894 articulated the principal design for the façade of the Museum's entrance wing; and the landscape architect Frederick Law Olmsted, in whose Central Park the Museum is situated.

The Museum's earliest mandate focused on the formation of a collection that would present to the public works of art of the highest quality from earliest times to the present. The Museum grew, and its holdings became a collection of collections, a living encyclopedia of the history of art. During the twentieth century the present has become recent and the recent has become the past. Thus, the Museum's collections of nineteenth-century American and European art—once "modern"—are displayed in appropriate historical contexts in The American Wing and in The Andre Meyer Galleries.

Today, the Museum's collection of twentieth-century art is international, and it comprises painting and sculpture, design and architecture, photography, drawings, and prints. Various aspects of this collection had been originally gathered and administered by several curatorial departments, but as the Museum's twentieth-century holdings grew, it became apparent to the trustees that a new, unified curatorial department should be established. This was done in 1967, and Henry Geldzahler was named its first curator. Geldzahler resigned in 1977 to become New York's Commissioner of Cultural Affairs, and in 1978, he was succeeded at the Museum by Thomas B. Hess, the department's first chairman, who died tragically the same year. In June 1979 the present chairman was appointed, and he assumed his duties the following December.

REPRODUCED in this publication are paintings executed from 1945 to 1985. A companion volume illustrates paintings from the previous four decades. Both selections can only suggest the extent of the Metropolitan's holdings in twentieth-century art, which the Museum began to collect when George A. Hearn, a trustee, established two endowment funds, one in 1906 in his own name and the other in 1911 in the name of his son, for the acquisition of paintings by living American artists. Over the years the purchasing power of the income derived from these two funds has diminished severely. Nevertheless, they have made possible, many years after George Hearn's death, the acquisition of several notable works, including Charles Sheeler's *Water* (1945), purchased in 1949; Jackson Pollock's *Autumn Rhythm* (1950), purchased in 1957; as well as paintings by Josef Albers, Stuart Davis, Franz Kline, and Yves Tanguy, purchased at the time they were painted. These American acquisitions reflect and confirm the discerning taste of the late Robert Beverly Hale, former curator of American paintings and sculpture, who was also responsible for choosing Edwin W. Dickinson's *Ruin at Daphne* (1943–53), a memorial gift in the name of Edward Joseph Gallagher III, and Robert Motherwell's late *Elegy to the Spanish Republic* (1961).

Between 1970 and 1977 Henry Geldzahler recommended to the trustees several acquisitions, among them Clyfford Still's lyric abstraction (1946) and Mark Rothko's *Untitled (Number 16)* of 1960, purchased with Hearn funds, and David Hockney's view of Mount Fuji, purchased in 1972, the year it was painted, with funds generously supplied by Mrs. Arthur Hays Sulzberger. In 1975 Milton Avery's *White Rooster* (1947) and Balthus's *Nude in Front of a Mantel* (1955) were acquired, the former a gift of Joyce Blaffer von Bothmer in memory of her parents and the latter a bequest of Robert Lehman, a trustee of the Museum.

Other paintings by European artists reproduced here are Max Beckmann's *Beginning* (1949), the bequest of Miss Adelaide Milton de Groot in 1967; Dali's *Crucifixion* (1954), given to the Museum by trustee Chester Dale a year after it was painted; Picasso's *Seated Musketeer and Standing Nude* (1968), gift of A. L. and Blanche Levine in 1981; and Georg Baselitz's *Man of Faith* (1983), given by Barbara and Eugene Schwartz in 1985.

Lila Acheson Wallace had many philanthropic interests, all of which continue to benefit the public. At the Metropolitan Museum she is responsible for the Galleries of Egyptian Art as well as the new wing for twentieth-century art, both named in her honor. Mrs. Wallace's chief personal interest was flowers and gardens, reflected in the continuing display of flowers in the Great Hall of the Museum and in the recent restoration of Claude Monet's garden at Giverny. She therefore particularly admired Stanley Spencer's *King's Cookham Rise* (1947), the first painting by this British artist to enter the Museum's collection. The most recent work reproduced in this book is Kitaj's *John Ford on His Deathbed,* painted in 1984, the year of Mrs. Wallace's death, and acquired by the Museum in 1986 with funds given by her.

Museums often lack the specific funds necessary to purchase a desired single work of art. Mrs. Wallace realized this. She and Mr. and Mrs. Andrew Saul added to the Hearn funds to make possible the acquisition of Philip Guston's *The Street* (1977); she also supplemented Hearn funds for the purchase of James Rosenquist's *House of Fire* (1981). And, in 1982, nine members of the Museum's Visiting Committee for 20th Century Art joined Mrs. Wallace in making possible the acquisition of Roy Lichtenstein's *Stepping Out* (1978).

BECAUSE of chronic lack of funds, the Metropolitan's purchases of twentieth-century works of art have been limited, and the continuing development of the collection cannot rely on purchases alone. The collaboration and concern of private collectors, artists, and dealers are essential, and, fortunately, the Museum has many friends. In 1982, with her gift of Willem de Kooning's *Attic* (1949), Muriel Kallis Newman reaffirmed the commitment of her entire collection to the Museum, of which she is an honorary trustee. In 1985 The Mark Rothko Foundation, Inc. complemented the Museum's existing holdings of his work with a gift of four paintings and nine drawings ranging in date from 1943 to 1969. The Bernhill Fund has made possible the acquisition of two paintings by Cy Twombly, one of which is the 1970 composition reproduced here, and Romare Bearden's six-panel *The Block* (1971) was the gift of Mr. and Mrs. Samuel Shore. Unfortunately, the Museum's representation of modern art of the other Americas is weak, but we hope that the recent gift of Fernando Botero's *Dancing in Colombia* (1980) will stimulate other gifts of paintings by artists from beyond the territorial confines of the United States.

THE SELECTION of paintings reproduced here suggests that by the middle of this century national distinctions in art had ceased to have much meaning. Josef Albers, a Master at the Bauhaus in Germany, came to the United States in 1933, while Yves Tanguy, a Surrealist in France, came in 1939; both painters died in Connecticut. Max Beckmann, the foremost German artist of our time, started his triptych *Beginning* in Amsterdam and completed it in St. Louis before settling in New York. Willem de Kooning, born in Rotterdam, was twenty-two years old in 1926 when he arrived in Hoboken, New Jersey. Salvador Dali lived in Paris and New York before returning to live in Spain; Pablo Picasso, another Spaniard, remained in France. The American painter Cy Twombly has lived in Rome since 1957, and R. B. Kitaj has been in London for more than thirty years. Balthus, born in Paris of Silesian parents, was raised in Berlin and Geneva, worked in France and Italy, and now resides in Switzerland. Fernando Botero, a Colombian, has worked in New York and now lives in France and Italy. David Hockney, an Englishman, travels extensively but regards Los Angeles as his home.

A selection limited to twenty-eight paintings by twenty-six artists executed over a period of four decades cannot begin to indicate the scope of the Museum's holdings. It does suggest, however, the healthy variety and international intent of the modern collection. Similar selections could and should be made. However, several serious lacunae continue to exist: for instance, no paintings by Ernst Ludwig Kirchner, Alberto Giacometti, or Jasper Johns are as yet in the Museum's collection.

SINCE 1971 the architectural firm of Kevin Roche John Dinkeloo & Associates has been responsible for the completion of a master plan conceived by the Museum and the City of New York to make available to the public the Metropolitan's comprehensive collections. Continuing a tradition of collaboration, the city, its mayor, and his commissioners have shared in a splendid fashion with the Museum, its curators, and its architects all phases of the planning and execution of the master plan.

The opening of the new Lila Acheson Wallace Wing reconfirms the Museum's commitment to the art of the present time. The wing, named for the co-founder of *Reader's Digest,* offers approximately 40,000 square feet of space for the display of twentieth-century art. The galleries survey in depth the Museum's growing collection, providing a frame of reference against which temporary exhibitions will be mounted. The wing also contains curatorial offices and rooms for study and storage. The Iris and B. Gerald Cantor Roof Garden contributes 10,000 additional square feet for the installation of sculpture out-of-doors on the new wing's roof, where it may be viewed against the panoramic backdrop of Central Park and the New York skyline.

In the Lila Acheson Wallace Wing the chronological installation of the permanent collection, which begins with the year 1900, is located in galleries on the first floor, where there is also a special gallery devoted to design and architecture. The thirty-foot-high Mezzanine Court for indoor sculpture is joined by two smaller galleries, each designed for works of art more intimate in scale. Installations in the skylit galleries on the second floor are devoted primarily to painting from 1940 to the present. The wing also includes several spaces for temporary exhibitions, including a large hall on the first floor and a smaller gallery on the second.

THE PAINTINGS reproduced in this publication appear in a chronological sequence. The accompanying details illuminate only one aspect of a painting, but it is hoped that they bring the painter closer to the reader.

William S. Lieberman

SHEELER: *Water,* 1945

Oil on canvas, 24 x 29¹/₈ in.
Arthur Hoppock Hearn Fund, 1949
(49.128)

CONTROVERSY ENGENDERED by the Armory Show of 1913 sparked the dialogue concerning the nature of an "American" art. The antagonists aligned themselves into two groups. The Regionalists—conservative artists who decried what they saw as the corrupting influence of European modern art—fiercely defended the moral rectitude of the American rural heartland. The second group, which gathered around the photographer Alfred Stieglitz and his gallery, 291, sought to incorporate the new modernist vocabulary into American culture, participating in what Oliver Larkin called "the domestication of distortion." Charles Sheeler was a key figure in this discourse.

Water, a depiction of one of the dams built for the Tennessee Valley Authority, is a powerful rendering of an American scene in a style marked by geometric precision and clarity, which betrays not only the influence of Cubism and Futurism but also Sheeler's experience as a photographer. The architecture has the streamlined look of the American "Moderne" style; the windows, the facade, and even the cast shadow have been manipulated to emphasize the formal properties of the shapes rather than the picturesque nuances of locale. Like several of his contemporaries, Sheeler came to believe that 20th-century landscape was that of industry, whose distinctive architecture and machinery demonstrated the ingenuity of man and his ability to harness the power of nature for his purposes. This belief marks a distinct break with the subliminal tradition of 18th- and 19th-century American and European landscape painting, in which man appears incidental to God, the universe, and nature.

In 1945, when this painting was finished, Sheeler completed three years' employment at the Metropolitan Museum, where he photographed objects in the Museum's collection. These photographs provide a fascinating study of the way his interpretive eye recorded works by other artists.

Lowery S. Sims

10

STILL: *Untitled (PH-384),* 1946

Oil on canvas, 61¾ x 44½ in.
George A. Hearn Fund and Arthur
Hoppock Hearn Fund, 1977 (1977.174)

BY HIS OWN ACCOUNT Clyfford Still's
first trip to New York in 1925 was a dis-
appointment, although he stayed long
enough to visit the Metropolitan Museum and the Art Students League. He
returned to the state of Washington,
where he completed his undergraduate
studies in art in 1933 and received a
master's degree in 1935. He moved to
San Francisco in 1941, and in 1943 he
went to Richmond, Virginia, where

he taught art until 1945, when he returned to New York City. He was soon
engaged for a one-man exhibition at
Peggy Guggenheim's gallery, Art of
This Century, and also made the ac-
quaintance of the young Abstract Expressionist painters. In their quest for a
mythic content embodied in abstract
form, these artists had begun to dis-
card the Surrealist-inspired biomorphic
shapes and Cubist structures that had
characterized their work during the late
1930s and early 1940s.

In this painting of 1946, Still con-
tinues to explore the formal possibilities of amorphous, jagged applications
of pigment, which had begun to figure
in his work as early as 1942–43. He jux-
taposes the different areas of color like
interlocking pieces of a puzzle, and he
gives the flat surface an allover treatment rather than a centralized composition. Still's colors are deep and rich;
small swatches of lighter or darker hues
appear at the juncture of larger areas.
There is little contrast in the intensity
of the colors, so that the entire composition seems to be compressed against
the surface of the painting. The pigment has been applied thickly with a
palette knife, creating a highly visible
surface of short, energetic "touches."
In Still's paintings of the 1950s, this
mottled surface would evolve into
discrete masses of color that dominate
the large, more vertically oriented compositions.

Lowery S. Sims

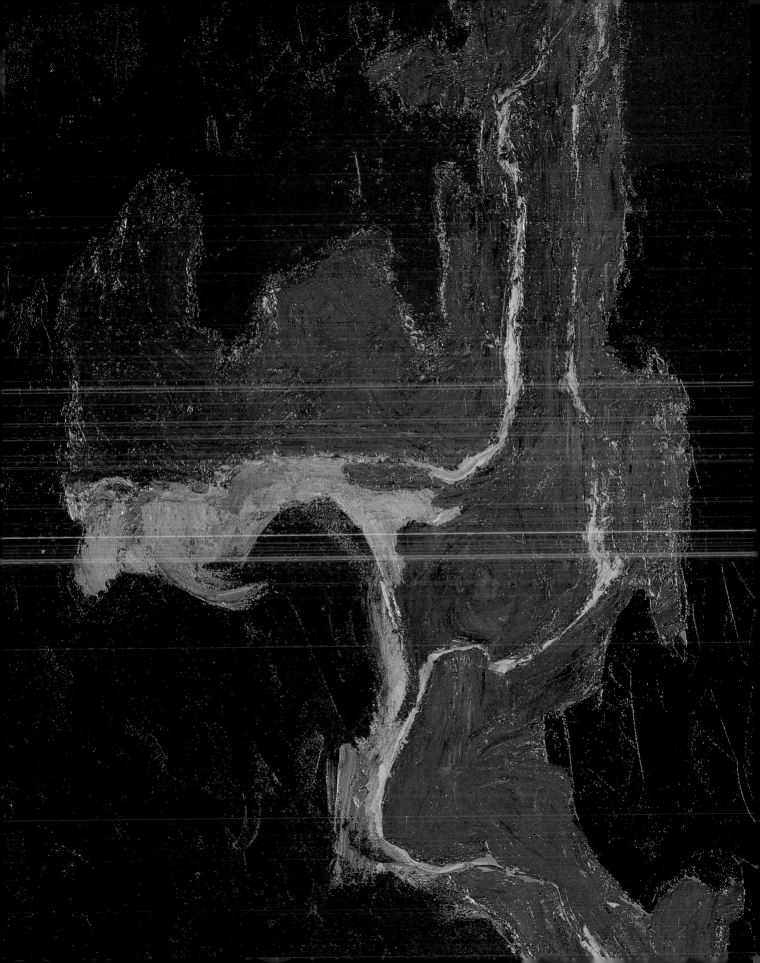

AVERY: *White Rooster,* 1947

Oil on canvas, 61 ½ x 50 ¾ in.
Gift of Joyce Blaffer von Bothmer, in
memory of Mr. and Mrs. Robert Lee Blaffer,
1975 (1975.210)

MILTON AVERY's subjects are appeal-
ing in their familiarity—serene land-
scapes, expansive seascapes, and
intimate studies of family and friends.
They are painted simply, with humor
and gentleness, and they delight the
eye and lift the spirit. Color is Avery's
primary means of expression, and his
use of it reflects the influence of Henri
Matisse. Unusual shades of pink, pur-
ple, orange, green, yellow, and blue,

all close in value, color the interlocking
shapes that tightly structure the composition. As in Matisse's work, these
bold planes can be perceived alter-
nately as flat and as three-dimensional.
Avery has applied paint in thin, feath-
ery brushstrokes that enliven the delicate surface.

Within each painting color vacil-
lates between naturalistic description
and arbitrary fancy. In *White Rooster*
two small brown chicks and a plump
rooster peck at the rose-pink ground,
oblivious to its unnatural hue. Beyond
them a wooded hill of light pink curves
gracefully along the orange-peach horizon; its two strips of green trees confront a large, bright-blue tree in the

middle ground. Avery blends reality
and fantasy effortlessly to produce a
whimsical and surprisingly tranquil
scene. His mastery of composition en-
ables us to enjoy this amusing narrative
without losing sight of the painting's
inherent abstractness.

Throughout his career Avery fol-
lowed an independent course that wove
a balanced path between abstraction
and representation. His paintings inspired a slightly later generation of
Abstract Expressionists—most impor-
tantly Mark Rothko (see pages 36 and
37)—and Color Field painters in their
own explorations of color and space.

Lisa Mintz Messinger

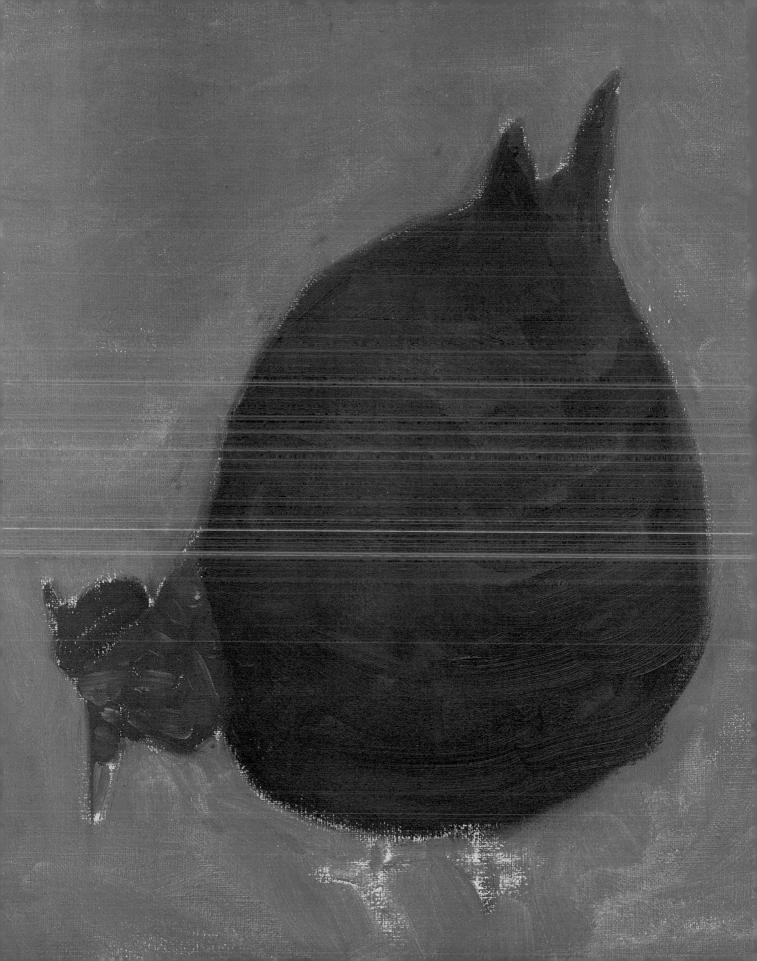

SPENCER:
King's Cookham Rise, 1947

Oil on canvas, 20 x 30 in.
Purchase, Lila Acheson Wallace Gift, 1981
(1981.193)

APART FROM EXPERIENCES gained during both world wars, three principal sources nourished the visionary art of the British painter Stanley Spencer: his happy childhood in the small town of Cookham on the Thames; the Bible, from which he transformed episodes into modern allegories; and the intensely felt joys and frustrations of his domestic life.

Spencer is best known as a painter of human figures in dramatic confron-tations, and he often worked in series devoted to specific themes. *King's Cookham Rise* was painted in 1947 as a single work between two such series, "Ship Building on the Clyde" and "The Resurrection." The former was a wartime commission and a celebration of industry; the latter was Spencer's fi-nal and most prolonged interpretation of the Easter theme. *King's Cookham Rise* seems to represent a joyous, quiet respite between the theatricality of the two series.

The village of Cookham in Berk-shire remained for Spencer a kind of paradise, and after the Second World War he returned there to live. Its rural surroundings are romantically and nos-talgically remembered in many of his paintings. This one describes a simple garden, each detail of which is lovingly and painstakingly rendered. The season is summer, when flowers and foliage are at their best and the weath-er is most conducive to painting out-of-doors.

This is one of Spencer's most beautifully patterned compositions, with a rich and wonderfully varied car-pet of flowers, foliage, fences, hedges, and shadows, and it anticipates his later interest in the textures of clothing and fabrics. The density of the brush-strokes is concentrated, and the appli-cation of paint is almost pointillist in technique.

William S. Lieberman

BECKMANN: *Beginning,* 1949

Oil on canvas; triptych, center panel 69 x 59
in.; side panels each 65 x 33¼ in.
Bequest of Miss Adelaide Milton de Groot
(1876–1967), 1967 (67.187.53a–c)

THE THEME THAT CONNECTS the three
panels of *Beginning,* the most auto-
biographical of Max Beckmann's ten
triptychs, is childhood.

The central panel shows a play-
room where a little boy in military costume brandishes a sword as he mightily
rides a rocking horse. The noise he
makes has alarmed his parents, who
have climbed up to inspect his attic
kingdom. The mother, behind the lad-
der, expresses concern while the father
raises a hand to admonish and restrain.
More prominently placed is the figure
of a girl, perhaps an older sister or
someone not yet met. She reclines,

limp as a doll, and her precocious phys-
icality is in contrast to her childlike
self-amusement as she blows blue bub-
bles from a pipe. Between the boy and
the girl sits an old woman, reading. We
see only her head and newspaper, and
from other Beckmann paintings we rec-
ognize her as his grandmother. At the
top right, a proscenium with a small
red curtain exposes part of a nursery
stage on which stands a puppet clown,
strangely bearded and quite ugly.

The left and right panels of
Beginning also present interior scenes,
and in them Beckmann summons
other vivid memories of his childhood.
At left, the boy costumed as a king
watches a blind hurdy-gurdy grinder,
whose tunes must sound celestial, since
seraphim appear as he plays. The boy's
garlanded consort stares only at herself.

In the right panel, a schoolroom
includes a globe and a bust of some

classical philosopher. The tall teacher,
hand in pocket, stoops over his students. One boy, face to the wall and
arms raised, is being punished, while
his classmates sit more comfortably at
their desks. Two, however, are also
naughty. They turn to look at us as they
pass between them a crude drawing of
a naked woman.

In his diary of 1946 Beckmann recorded the genesis of *Beginning,* which
he first called *L'Enfance* and *Jeunesse.*
He wrote to himself: "I just had a
ridiculous and unpleasant dream in
which somehow Puss 'n Boots played a
role which made me look really ridiculous." In the central panel of his triptych Beckmann paints a different
ending to the fairy tale as Puss 'n Boots
hangs upside down, suspended from
its spurs.

William S. Lieberman

18

DE KOONING: *Attic,* 1949

Oil, enamel, newspaper transfer on canvas,
61⅞ x 81 in.
Jointly owned by The Metropolitan
Museum of Art and Muriel Kallis Newman,
in honor of her son Glenn David Steinberg,
The MURIEL KALLIS STEINBERG NEWMAN
Collection, 1982 (1982.16.3)

IN HIS REFUSAL to abandon representa-
tional subject matter—primarily voluptuous women—Willem de Kooning
always veered from the mainstream of
Abstract Expressionism, a movement
in which he was nevertheless a leader.
Between 1946 and 1949, however, he
produced a series of highly abstract
black-and-white paintings that culminated in this early masterpiece, *Attic.*

The biomorphic symbols he devised,
like those of his friend Arshile Gorky,
cannot be seen as figures per se, but
they do allude to the curves and forms
of human anatomy. Such complex
compositions explore the positive-
negative relationships of form and
space. In *Attic* the web of white shapes
is so dense that the black background
on which they are situated virtually
disappears.

De Kooning's palette of black and
white, with touches of red and yellow,
was determined in part by the avail-
ability of inexpensive commercial
enamel paint. Although restricted in
his use of color, de Kooning displays
virtuosity in his sensuous, expressive
handling of paint, surface, and line.
Thomas B. Hess, the late art critic who
was de Kooning's friend, poetically

described the painting as "ruffled,
talc-soft whites, which turn tawny as
hooking black lines fold them." Its gestural brushwork and dynamic allover
composition exemplify the new visual
language adopted by the Abstract Expressionist painters. De Kooning rou-
tinely made revisions on his canvases,
and *Attic* was exhibited at two different stages of completion. To accelerate
the drying time of the paint, de Kooning blotted sheets of newspaper over
the wet canvas, and the surface bears
evidence of the transferred newsprint.
In the works that immediately follow
Attic, de Kooning resumed his use
of full color and soon returned to the
figurative imagery for which he is
best known.

Lisa Mintz Messinger

20

POLLOCK: *Autumn Rhythm*
(Number 30), 1950

Oil on canvas, 105 x 207 in.
George A. Hearn Fund, 1957 (57.92)

JACKSON POLLOCK's poured paintings are as visually potent today as when they first shocked the art world nearly forty years ago. Their appearance virtually shifted the focus of avant-garde art from Paris to New York, and their influence on the development of Abstract Expressionism—and on subsequent painting both here and abroad—was enormous.

To many, the large, eloquent canvases of 1950 are Pollock's greatest achievements. *Autumn Rhythm,* painted in October of that year, exemplifies the extraordinary balance between accident and control that Pollock maintained over his technique. The words *poured* and *dripped,* commonly used to describe his unorthodox creative process, which involved painting on unstretched canvas laid flat on the floor, hardly suggest the diversity of Pollock's movements (flicking, splattering, and dribbling), nor the lyrical, often spiritual compositions they produced.

Here, as in many of his other paintings, Pollock first created a complex linear skeleton with black paint. For this initial layer the paint was diluted so that it soaked into the length of unprimed canvas, thereby joining image and support inextricably. Over this black framework Pollock wove an intricate web of white, brown, and dark turquoise lines, which produce contrary visual rhythms and sensations: light and dark, thick and thin, heavy and buoyant, straight and curved, horizontal and vertical. Textural passages that contribute to the painting's complexity—like the pooled swirls where two colors meet, and like the wrinkled skins formed by the build-up of paint—are barely visible in the initial confusion of overlapping lines. Although Pollock's imagery is nonrepresentational, *Autumn Rhythm* is evocative of nature, not only in its title but also in its coloring, horizontal orientation, and sense of space and ground.

Lisa Mintz Messinger

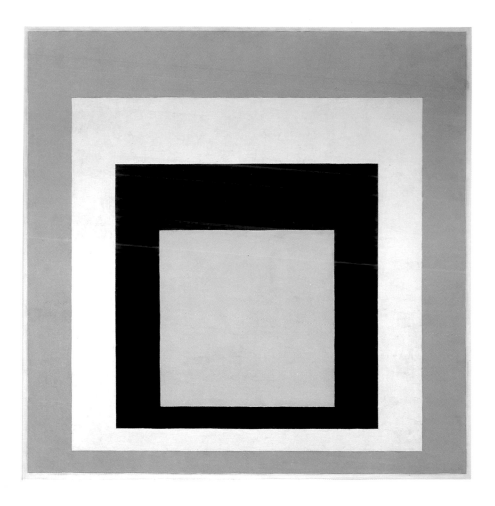

ALBERS: *Homage to the Square: Young,* 1951

Oil on masonite, 23⅝ x 23½ in.
George A. Hearn Fund, 1953 (53.174.1)

JOSEF ALBERS worked on a series of paintings exploring color and the spatial relationship of forms over a period of twenty-five years, beginning in 1948. These two works are part of that series, entitled collectively "Homage to the Square," in which Albers experimented with materials and with different solutions to the same problem, ideas that grew out of his association with the Bauhaus. Albers was on the faculty there from 1923 until 1933, when he emigrated to the United States. He then taught at Black Mountain College in North Carolina and later at Yale University.

Albers painted this series in oil, applying colors directly from the tube to the surface of the masonite. He then spread the pigment evenly with a palette knife, mixing the colors (where required) as he smeared them. In this series we can observe his preoccupation with the process of seeing—the ways in which the real world is perceived—and with techniques for creating the illusion of the third dimension on a flat surface. Whereas Western artists since the Renaissance have relied on such methods as diminishing the size of figures and objects and gradually fading their colors to convey a sense of depth, Albers achieves a similar effect by placing colors of specific intensity and hue next to each other. He kept exact records of the colors he used in each painting and determined the placement of each square and its color mathematically. In spite of this rather rigid, formal method and the limited visual means employed, Albers produced an extensive body of surprisingly varied statements on the same theme.

Lowery S. Sims

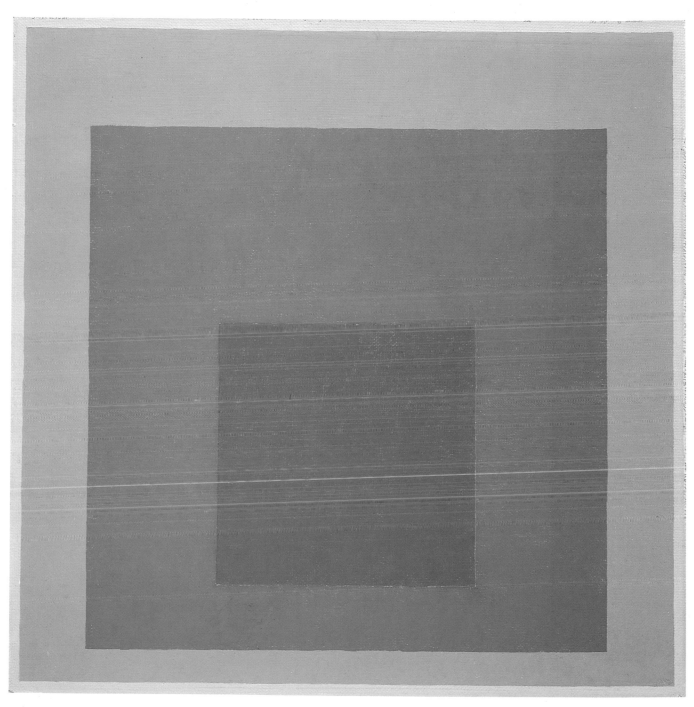

ALBERS: *Homage to the Square: Precinct,* 1951

Oil on masonite, 31 ¾ x 31 ¾ in.
George A. Hearn Fund, 1953 (53.174.2)

DICKINSON:
Ruin at Daphne, 1943–53

Oil on canvas, 48 x 60¼ in.
The Edward Joseph Gallagher III Memorial
Collection, Gift of Edward J. Gallagher, Jr.,
1955 (55.13.1)

THE REALIZATION of certain paintings
is the result of slow development and
constant change. Edwin Dickinson's
spectacular panorama *Ruin at Daphne*
was painted over a period of nine or ten
years. His revisions were photographed
at different stages, and as they are re-
viewed, their sequence unfolds in cine-
matic fashion. The final state of the
painting, which he considered unfinished, combines and distills a rich variety of visual experiences.

Dickinson himself offered no specific explanation of his subject, but
the origins of its imagery derive from
accumulated sources. As he painted,
his composition grew more and more
complex. He borrowed from the ruins
of at least two classical sites to create a
new setting—ambiguous, mysterious,
and his own.

"*Ruin at Daphne,* the Metropolitan's painting, grew out of an interest
in Roman architecture when I was living in Arles," the artist wrote. The
identifiable architectural elements,
however, stand elsewhere. The round
Temple of Venus at the upper left remains intact today at Baalbek, where
the spiral column prominent in the
foreground is also found, but in Dickinson's painting the Corinthian capital

supports nothing. He also incorporates
and expands three huge vaults that
were originally tall bays on an interior
aisle in the ruined Basilica of Constan-
tine in the Roman Forum.

In addition, Dickinson studied
the composition and technique of
Leonardo's *Adoration of the Magi,* also
an unfinished picture. In its background appear similar steps that as-
cend to nowhere and a small rearing
horse, which Dickinson, in his own
painting, floats above the basin of a
fountain. The underpainting of
Leonardo's *Adoration* is drawn in red-
dish brown, and the unfinished edges
of Dickinson's picture reveal a similar
method.

William S. Lieberman

DAVIS: *Semé,* 1953

Oil on canvas, 52 x 40 in.
George A. Hearn Fund, 1953 (53.90)

AS THE FIRST MAJOR EXHIBITION of modern European art in this country, the Armory Show of 1913 had a major impact on American art. For Stuart Davis, then nineteen years old and already a practicing artist with five of his own watercolors in the show, the contact with Post-Impressionism, Cubism, and Futurism provided exciting new visual possibilities that would guide and inspire his work through the next four decades.

Davis found a formula suited to his own visual explorations in the conventions of Synthetic Cubism, in which the forms of objects are depicted as overlapping geometric shapes. Through his concentration on still life, including the popular images of a burgeoning consumer society, Davis indicated the path for a uniquely American art that broke completely with traditional subject matter. In *Semé* we see Davis at the peak of his creative powers. The bright, articulated forms that seem to be numbers, letters, and symbols that resemble musical notation summarize his principal interests, those two seminal inspirations for much of American art—advertising and jazz.

Although Davis's use of typographical elements during this period has been seen as less systematic than in his earlier works, he gives the viewer clues to decipher the work's powerful visual impact. The artist noted in an interview that *semé* in French means *strewn,* as the composition is, in this case, with vivid greens and blues that create electrically charged visual vibrations with the contrasting reds and oranges. The word ANY is meant to indicate the equality of all the elements in the picture, and *Eydeas* in the lower left is a wonderfully onomatopoeic fusion of the two words *eye* and *ideas.*

Davis was a tireless propagandizer for abstract art, which continued to face strong resistance until well after the Second World War. In this capacity he paved the way for the acceptance that Abstract Expressionists were able to attain in the 1950s.

Lowery S. Sims

DALI: *Crucifixion,* 1954

Oil on canvas, 76 ½ x 48 ¾ in.
Gift of The Chester Dale Collection,
1955 (55.5)

AS WE APPROACH the end of the 20th century, an age that has so often denied spiritual values, it is a surprise to see any painting that portrays the Crucifixion. The most familiar description of this event, central to the Christian faith, is in the Gospel according to Saint Luke, who remembered that Christ "was lifted up before their eyes, and a cloud took Him from their sight." Salvador Dali's representation, not unexpectedly, conforms neither to Luke nor to the pictorial tradition that persisted throughout the Middle Ages and the Renaissance.

Dali has never been modest about himself or his art. Indeed, he has courted notoriety during his entire career. During the early 1930s in Paris, he quickly gained a reputation as the most eccentric as well as the youngest member of the group of Surrealist poets and artists led by André Breton.

In his religious paintings of the 1950s, however, Dali reaffirmed his own Christian faith. When the *Crucifixion* was first exhibited in Rome, the Vatican proclaimed it one of the most significant creations of religious art in our time, and the artist must surely have been pleased. He declared that the metaphysical concept of this tall, imposing picture was based on a treatise on cubic form written by Juan de Herrera, a 17th-century Spanish architect. When the picture was given to the Metropolitan Museum in 1955, Dali announced: "My ambition is to continue the tradition of Spanish aesthetic thought in its diverse manifestations."

Dali described the woman who gazes at the body of Christ as "a figure of human proportions which has the prescience, in its contemplation, of the grandeur of the divine drama." But exactly who is she, folded into rich fabrics of cloth, standing beneath Christ's cross? She is none of the three Marys; instead, she is "Gala," the muse of Dali's art. Born Helena Dimitriovnie Diakonova, Gala was a short, determined Russian beauty who was especially proud of her shapely back. In 1917 she met the French poet Paul Éluard and later married him. In 1929, however, she encountered Dali and subsequently became his wife.

William S. Lieberman

TANGUY: *The Mirage of Time,* 1954

Oil on canvas, 39 x 32 in.
George A. Hearn Fund, 1955 (55.95)

IT WAS THE SURREALIST artists who admitted the world of dreams into the repertoire of modern painting. The French-born artist Yves Tanguy in particular took the inner landscape of man's imagination and made it the focal point of his creative output. Tanguy claimed that seeing one of Giorgio de Chirico's paintings in the window of an art dealer in Paris in the early 1920s was the catalyst for his eventual involvement in art and Surrealism.

Tanguy's earliest paintings feature amoebalike shapes—not unlike the biomorphic transformations of Joan Miró—set in mysterious locales in which the horizon line looms ominously. By the 1930s these shapes had developed into Tanguy's characteristic rock or bone forms, which evoke a certain ambiguity about their exact nature. We are tempted to read anatomical and landscape elements into these forms, however, much as we do with stones on the beach and clouds in the sky. This use of free association, dubbed the "paroid critical" method by Salvador Dali, is the basis for much Surrealist creative endeavor because it serves to free the viewer from the tyranny of the narratives that dominated academic painting. The Surrealists wanted viewers to initiate their own interpretations of the visual elements presented by the artist.

Like many avant-garde artists of his generation, Tanguy left Europe at the start of the Second World War. He married the American painter Kay Sage in 1940, and two years later they moved to Woodbury, Connecticut, where Tanguy executed *The Mirage of Time* a year before his death in 1955.

Lowery S. Sims

BALTHUS: *Nude in Front of a Mantel*, 1955

Oil on canvas, 75 x 64 ½ in.
Robert Lehman Collection, 1975
(1975.1.155)

THE CAREER of the French figurative painter Balthus spans more than half a century, from the late 1920s to the present. His paintings aim at classical order and a refined aestheticism unrelated to contemporary art and life. Composed in an archaizing manner, they are reminiscent of early Renaissance painting, with a surface handling derived from Courbet. His best-known subjects are Parisian street scenes, probing psychological portraits, and interiors with adolescent girls.

Balthus has always been unusually susceptible to his surroundings, using them as the settings for his paintings. In 1953 he moved to an abandoned chateau, Chassy, in the hilly region of Morvan in central France, and its finely restored rooms replaced his earlier interiors as the backdrops of his works. In this large painting we see one of Chassy's ground-floor rooms. As usual, Balthus constructs his composition with the precision of an architect. The underlying grid of squares, along which all forms are aligned, is still visible under the thinly scumbled paint.

Singular in this work is the even, clear light that fills the bare room. It illuminates the sky-blue and white wallpaper, the off-white, beige, and brown wainscoting, and the ornate, gray Louis-Philippe marble mantel. Gazing into the blackened, yellow-framed mirror on the mantel is a statuesque nude whose form and stance echo the shape of the pale-blue pitcher before her. Seen in profile with one foot planted firmly in front of the other, she evokes a figure from an Egyptian relief.

Balthus found the inspiration for this nude in a magazine illustration. The figure of the girl is life-size, measuring just under five feet tall, but by lowering the mantel to the height of her waist, Balthus imbues her with an amazing monumentality.

Sabine Rewald

ROTHKO: *Untitled (Number 13),* 1958

Oil, acrylic, with powdered pigments on
canvas, 95³/₈ x 81³/₈ in.
Gift of the Mark Rothko Foundation, Inc.,
1985 (1985.63.5)

ABSTRACT EXPRESSIONISM encom-
passes two very different sensibilities:
one, exemplified by de Kooning and
Pollock (see pages 20 and 22), characterized by energetic brushwork and
rhythmic compositions; the other, rep-
resented here by two paintings of Mark
Rothko, contemplative in tone, result-
ing from subtle color harmonies and
relatively static compositions made up
of a few simple elements.

By 1950 Rothko developed the
compositional format that he was to
use, with refinements and variations,
for the next twenty years of his life. In
these completely abstract works, color
and shape replace traditional narrative
content and figurative imagery. Two
or three horizontal bars of varying size
and color dominate the large, primarily vertical canvases, and they appear
to hover on the picture surface. This effect is produced in part by the "halo"
created around the horizontal bands as
they overlap the background color. It
is also enhanced by the translucency of
the paint, which was so diluted that
it actually saturated and stained the
fibers of the canvas. Although Rothko
minimized the tactile nature of the
medium, these paintings still retain a
painterly quality in their subtle brushwork and in the ragged edges of the
forms.

In Rothko's oeuvre color varies
greatly, and it evokes a full range of
emotions: from the bright, joyous primary hues used in *Untitled (Number
13)* of 1958, to the dark, brooding
purples, reds, and browns of *Untitled
(Number 16)* of 1960, and, ultimately,
to the stark, monochromatic grays,
browns, and blacks of his last paintings, many of which were done on
paper a year or two before his suicide.
Because of their large size, these
canvases literally surround the viewer,
engaging him in silent dialogue.

Lisa Mintz Messinger

ROTHKO: *Untitled
(Number 16), 1960*

Oil on canvas, 102 x 119½ in.
Arthur Hoppock Hearn Fund, George A.
Hearn Fund, and Hugo Kastor Fund, 1971
(1971.14)

KLINE: *Black, White, and Gray*, 1959

Oil on canvas, 105 x 78 in.
George A. Hearn Fund, 1959 (59.165)

FRANZ KLINE painted his first large-scale black-and-white compositions in the winter of 1949–50. Their genesis was a group of small abstract drawings in black and white paint and black ink, which he projected with a Bell-opticon machine to create compositions that matched the heroic proportions of those produced by his Abstract Expressionist contemporaries. Born in Pennsylvania, Kline attended art school in London during the late 1930s and thus missed the seminal years of interaction among the future members of the New York School. When he returned to the United States and set up a studio in New York City, he was eventually attracted to the gestural and automatist interests of the American avant-garde.

In his mature work, exemplified by *Black, White, and Gray,* Kline manifested several prevailing theories (if we may call them that) of Abstract Expressionism. The reduction of his palette to predominantly black and white has been seen as an indication of his interest in calligraphy, his search for analogies between the sparse spontaneity of the Zen artist and the cultivation of accident and chance by the Abstract Expressionists. But Kline was specific in asserting that his work was not to be read as mere typographical renderings —although he did on occasion paint on telephone-book pages and newsprint—but as carefully considered visual relationships between different areas of black, white, and, in this case, gray. Kline noted that the white areas were not merely sections of a background left visible after the black and gray had been painted but were created as deliberately as the other colors, thus modifying the usual distinctions between figure and background, between positive and negative areas. The freely articulated brushstrokes, like those of de Kooning and Motherwell (see pages 20 and 40), are an important part of the work's visual presence. They not only mark the progress of the creative process as it is enacted directly on the canvas but also provide access to the artist's inner consciousness. Kline, like Motherwell, filled his canvases with large, monolithic forms that evoke architectural and landscape references. The artist himself pointed out figural associations that had been distilled from the more realist phase of his development.

Lowery S. Sims

MOTHERWELL: *Elegy to the Spanish Republic, 70,* 1961

Oil on canvas, 69 x 114 in.
Anonymous Gift, 1965 (65.247)

IN 1948 Robert Motherwell sketched a small black-and-white drawing for magazine reproduction, to accompany Harold Rosenberg's poem "The Bird for Every Bird." The publication was never realized, but the following year he painted a larger version of the image, which he titled *At Five in the Afternoon,* after a repeating phrase in a poem by Federico García Lorca. Both works evolved into an ongoing series of some one hundred painted variations on a theme the artist calls "Elegies to the Spanish Republic."

Initially inspired by the crisis of the Spanish Civil War, the real subject of Motherwell's "Elegies" is not any particular literary source or political event but rather a general meditation on life and death. Although specific paintings may express an individual spirit, or "tone voice," they remain a family group, related to one another by subject and by similarities in composition and format. In all paintings in the series, the horizontal white canvas is rhythmically divided by two or three freely drawn vertical bars and punctuated at various intervals by ovoid forms. These structural elements seem heraldic and are almost always painted in only black and white, the colors of mourning.

Motherwell's "Elegies" of the 1960s reflect his Abstract Expressionist affiliations in the gestural, painterly treatment of form, the rapid execution, and the integration of accidental effects, such as spattered paint. *Elegy to the Spanish Republic, 70* was executed on the floor rather than on an easel, in the manner of Jackson Pollock's earlier "poured" paintings (see page 22). The series that Motherwell began in 1948 culminated thirty years later in his *Reconciliation Elegy,* now in the National Gallery of Art, Washington, D.C.

Lisa Mintz Messinger

PICASSO: *Seated Musketeer and Standing Nude,* 1968

Oil on canvas, 63¾ x 51 in.
Jointly owned by The Metropolitan
Museum of Art and A. L. and Blanche
Levine, 1981 (1981.508)

THE MISCHIEVOUSLY HUMOROUS
Seated Musketeer and Standing Nude
was painted in November 1968, when
Pablo Picasso was eighty-seven years
old. The amatory overtones, exuberant
display of color, and virtuoso application of paint are characteristic of the
large body of works he produced in the
few years before his death. The figure
of a musketeer, alone or with nude
women, appears often in Picasso's late
work, just as the powerful minotaur

frequented Picasso's paintings, drawings, and prints during the 1930s. Both
musketeer and minotaur have been
interpreted as references to the artist.
In his later years Picasso apparently
preferred the less overtly sexual symbol
of the musketeer, whose reputation
is nonetheless that of a lady's man
and rogue, an ardent enjoyer of life.

This painting is reminiscent of
Picasso's artist and model series of the
1950s and 1960s. In *Seated Musketeer
and Standing Nude* the man is not in
the guise of an artist, but the relationship between the two figures remains
the same: the male represents reality,
the female, his elusive imagining. The
large, centrally placed, pipe-smoking
musketeer is strongly rendered, with
emphasis placed on his physical presence, gesture, and costume. In contrast, the voluptuous nude, crowded
into a narrow strip of canvas at the left,
is more tentatively painted, as if she
were only a thought in the musketeer's
mind.

Picasso enhances the frivolity of
the scene with a bright palette dominated by blue and accented with
touches of green, orange, red, and
pink. The paint is applied in thin
washes, with quick, sure strokes. The
circular forms representing a variety
of images—eyes, breasts, buttons,
toes, buckles, chair knobs—punctuate
the composition and provide visual
cohesion.

Lisa Mintz Messinger

TWOMBLY: *Untitled,* 1970

Oil and crayon on canvas, 61½ x 75 in.
Purchase, The Bernhill Fund Gift, 1984
(1984.70)

THE PHRASE "drawing into painting,"
which has been used to explain Jackson
Pollock's mature work, exactly describes this large abstraction by the
American artist Cy Twombly, who has
lived in Rome since 1957. In his highly
personal style, Twombly applies the
mediums and techniques of drawing—
in this case colored crayon used in a
calligraphic manner—on a painted

canvas surface. Unlike Pollock, whose
imagery was in part the result of
chance, Twombly maintains control
over the creative process by applying
pigment directly onto the surface in an
action akin to writing. His expressive
gesture is disciplined though spirited,
and he produces scribblings of remark-
able elegance and grace.

In this work seven horizontal
bands defined with crayon cross a
painted neutral background, which
covers the canvas evenly. These bands
of loosely coiled lines increase in size
and deepen in color as their rhythm
and intensity increase toward the bottom of the painting. Thus, the top
register offers a single meandering line

drawn in gray, while the lowest and
widest band presents an elaborate overlapping of multiple lines, some drawn
decisively in black and orange, others
rubbed into the background. This gra-
dation of size and hue creates a sense of
movement and depth, and in spite of
the deliberate absence of recognizable
imagery, there is a strong suggestion of
an autumnal landscape.

The painting is an exceptional
example of Twombly's later work, in
which color and line, devoid of repre-
sentational allusion, show him to be
a true heir to the first generation of
Abstract Expressionists.

Lisa Mintz Messinger

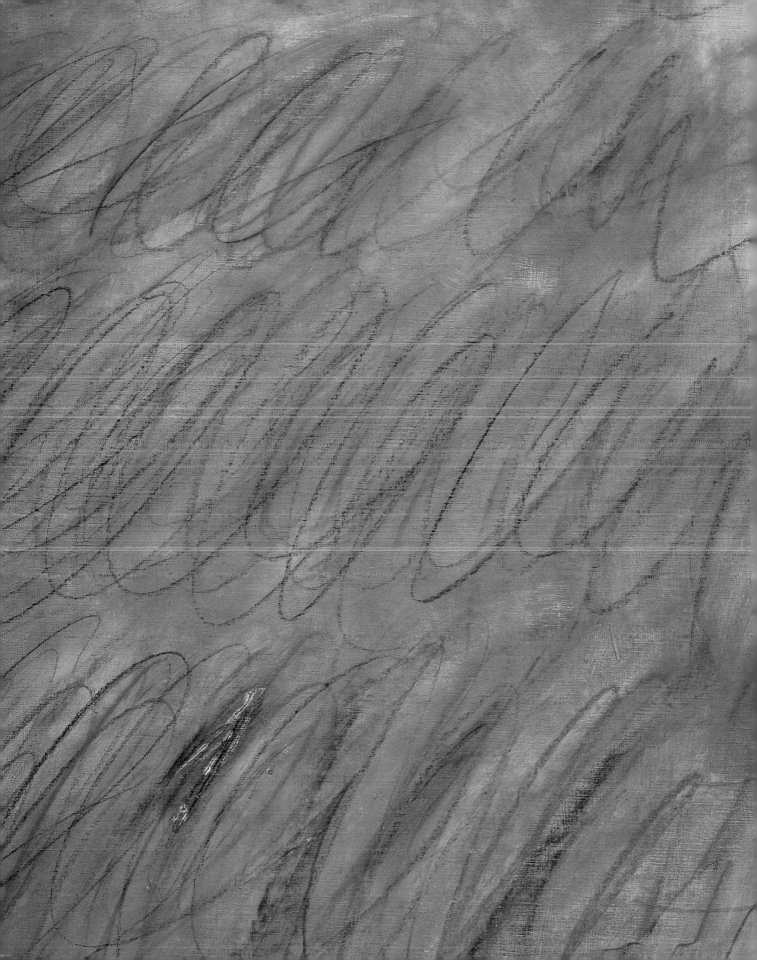

BEARDEN: *The Block,* 1971

Cut and pasted papers on masonite, overall
size: 4 x 18 ft.; six panels each 49 x 36 in.
Gift of Mr. and Mrs. Samuel Shore, 1978
(19/8.61.1–6)

THE BLOCK is a tribute to Harlem, a
neighborhood in New York City that
nurtured both the life and the work of
artist Romare Bearden. Although he
was born in Charlotte, North Carolina,
Bearden spent part of each year in New
York throughout his childhood. In
1940 he established his first studio in
Harlem at 306 West 125th Street, in
the same building with the artist Jacob
Lawrence and the poet-novelist Claude
McKay. During the 1940s Bearden was
active in the Harlem cultural commu-
nity, as part of the informal artists' or-
ganization known as the 306 Group
and as a member of the Harlem Artists
Guild.

Each of the six panels of *The Block*
presents an aspect of life in Harlem,
depicting such neighborhood institu-
tions as the Evangelical church, the
barber shop, or the corner grocery
store. Bearden takes artistic license in
revealing the private moments of tene-

ment life as well as the exuberant hu-
manity that exists in this prototypical
city block. His concern with social is-
sues reflects the influence of the German artist George Grosz, with whom
Bearden had studied at the Art Students League in New York in the 1930s.
The "cubist" character of Bearden's
cut-paper collage, a technique with
which he has become associated, results
from formal experimentation, the doc-
umentary impulse of Dadaist photo-
montage, and Bearden's own modern
vision, which matured during the
1940s and 1950s.

The original installation of this
work included a tape recording of street
sounds to enhance the viewer's visual
experience of the work, but even without this accompaniment we have a real
sense of the vitality of the scene.

Lowery S. Sims

Although David Hockney developed artistically in the London art scene of the late 1950s and remains a British subject, he has spent so much time in the United States over the last two decades—mostly in New York and Los Angeles—that he has inevitably had an effect on the American art world. Hockney has always manifested a strong figurative impulse in his work. As a student of art history, however, and a versatile technician who can work fluently in several mediums, Hockney has always combined this realism with a deft gestural touch derived from Abstract Expressionism and a lively sense of decoration. His work, particularly that of the 1960s, has shown an affinity to Pop Art, but he never succumbed to its consumerist and media-oriented obsessions.

Mount Fuji and Flowers demonstrates the artist's range. Hockney created this lyrical view of the legendary mountain with a floral arrangement on the occasion of his first visit to Japan in 1971. Hockney mimics the delicate washes of Color Field painting in the blue background and the dripping and running of thinned paint in the mountain itself. Then, as if to fend off the philistines convinced of the technical ineptitude of modern painters, Hockney places at the bottom of the composition a finely crafted depiction of white jonquils in a cinnabar-stained bamboo vase. The formal element of the ledge is familiar to us from Renaissance painting, as it serves to separate the different levels of reality—the mountain and the vase of flowers. With it Hockney reminds us of the inherent artifice involved in creating the illusion of three dimensions on a flat surface, a dilemma that has predicated much of the formal experimentation in modern art.

Lowery S. Sims

HOCKNEY: *Mount Fuji and Flowers,* 1972

Acrylic on canvas, 60 x 48 in.
Purchase, Mrs. Arthur Hays Sulzberger
Gift, 1972 (1972.128)

GUSTON: *The Street,* 1977

Oil on canvas, 69 x 110¾ in.
Purchase, Lila Acheson Wallace and Mr. and
Mrs. Andrew Saul Gifts, Gift of George A.
Hearn, by exchange, and Arthur Hoppock
Hearn Fund, 1983 (1983.457)

THIS MONUMENTAL PAINTING summarizes several raw and visceral themes that characterize Philip Guston's return to figurative subject matter in the late 1960s, after he had been for many years one of the most lyrical of the first-generation Abstract Expressionists. The painting's poignant narrative of confrontation, struggle, and uncertainty is as ambiguous as it is compelling, with precedents in his social commentaries painted during the 1930s and 1940s.

The composition of *The Street* is divided into three vertical sections, each depicting a different state of being—passive decay, violent aggression, and total confusion. At the right a large trash can is stuffed to overflowing with empty bottles, old strips of wood, a shoe, and other refuse. In the center a barrage of disembodied hairy paws juts out, holding trash-can lids as shields. These arms confront a jumble of interlocked skinny legs that seem to be thwarted by their own oversize shoes. Below, on the horizon line, which is the street itself, a pair of spiders sit poised for action.

Guston's work remained an intensely personal statement throughout its many transformations, often relying on his private iconography of images to convey the truth about the human condition and to express the artist's own inner fears and crises. As he wrote in 1974, his late paintings depict a "sort of Dante Inferno land." *The Street*'s unsettling color scheme of bright pink, red, and black and its crude style of painting add to the turmoil and despair.

Lisa Mintz Messinger

LICHTENSTEIN:
Stepping Out, 1978

Oil and magna on canvas, 86 x 70 in.
Purchase, Lila Acheson Wallace Gift,
Arthur Hoppock Hearn Fund, Arthur Lejwa
Fund in honor of Jean Arp and The Bernhill
Fund, Joseph H. Hazen Foundation, Inc.,
Samuel I. Newhouse Foundation, Inc.,
Walter Bareiss, Marie Bannon McHenry,
Louise Smith, and Stephen C. Swid Gifts,
1980 (1980.420)

ROY LICHTENSTEIN is considered one
of the founders of the movement
known as Pop Art, which recycled images and concepts from popular culture
in the context of "fine" art. Since
the 1960s, Lichtenstein has blown up
frames from romantic serials and war
sagas in a mechanical style derived
from the Benday dots of his comic-strip
sources. During the 1970s, however, he
began to enlarge his artistic vocabulary
to include more-or-less direct quotations from art history.

Lichtenstein himself has acknowl-
edged an affinity with Mondrian,
whose restricted palette of the three
primary colors and black and white he
adopted long ago. But critics have
noted the influence of Fernand Léger
as well, though it was only in the 1970s
that Lichtenstein began to incorporate
direct references to Léger's work in his
own. The young man in *Stepping Out,*
painted in 1978, is based on the left-
hand figure in Léger's 1944 composition *Three Musicians,* which Lichtenstein studied at the Museum of Modern
Art in New York. He has reversed the
original image of the man and borrowed his boutonnière from another.

Whereas most of Lichtenstein's
quotations tend to be relatively true to
his sources, in *Stepping Out* he has
provided the dapper young man with a
female companion of uncertain origin.
The dislocation of elements in this figure is Surrealist in spirit, calling to
mind the work of René Magritte during
the 1920s and that of Picasso during
the 1930s, particularly his *Bather Play-
ing Ball* of 1932 (also in the Museum of
Modern Art). This combination of art-
historical references from different eras
is typical of the provocative visual
statements that Lichtenstein has con-
sistently achieved, and it demonstrates
the artist's continuing preoccupation
with ready-made imagery.

Lowery S. Sims

52

BOTERO: *Dancing in Colombia,* 1980

Oil on canvas, 74 x 91 in.
Anonymous Gift, 1983 (1983.251)

FERNANDO BOTERO, the Colombian painter and sculptor, has invited us to a special occasion, perhaps a Saturday night when a change in dress and a bit of money can provide temporary release from the tedium of a week's routine. We join the patrons of a slightly seedy café to hear music and watch dancing. The evening promises potential adventure: Perhaps the rooms up-

stairs can be rented by the hour. That possibility is not painted, however, nor is the close atmosphere of the room, which must certainly combine the odors of sweat and tobacco, liquor and cheap cologne.

The space is crowded. A curtain of red cloth, the gathered folds of which can never drop, serves as a frame for the narrow stage on which an enormous amount of activity is concentrated. Curiously, no member of the band wears a convivial expression; with the exception of the flutist, each stares solemnly ahead. Stout, tightly suited, thick-necked, and standing, the six male musicians wear similar mustaches and hats. The seventh musician, a woman, is similarly thick-necked, and

one hopes that she is seated. All the members of the band look constrained. Like babies, the players seem to need a gentle hand to burp them.

Directly beneath the musicians but unseen by them, an inexplicably smaller couple dances. Shown in profile, their flat figures are like two elements of a child's toy that can be pulled from either left or right. The little man's clothing and expression match those of the taller musicians. His partner, with her hair and one leg flying, moves with greater abandon. The discarded cigarette butts add visual rhythms to the couple's dancing feet.

William S. Lieberman

ROSENQUIST:
House of Fire, 1981

Oil on canvas, 78 x 198 in.
Purchase, Arthur Hoppock Hearn Fund,
George A. Hearn Fund, and Lila Acheson
Wallace Gift, 1982 (1982.90.1a–c)

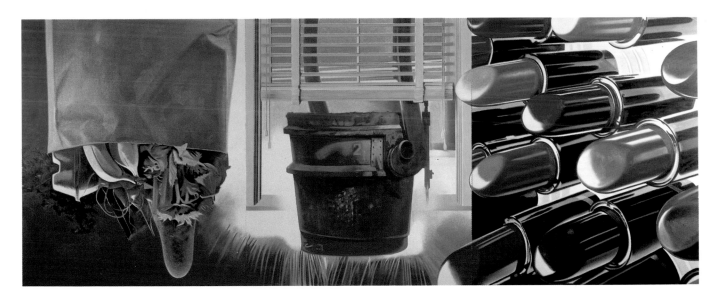

PAINTED BY James Rosenquist twenty years after his first Pop Art pictures, *House of Fire* exudes the same dynamism that characterizes his best work of the 1960s. It is a dramatic composition of heroic proportions and fiery coloration that is painted on three adjoining canvases. In contrast to his earlier paintings, where images were fragmented and overlapped, here the three unrelated motifs are presented whole within their individual panels.

As with all of Rosenquist's allegories, one must guess at the exact meaning of the realistically rendered and jarringly juxtaposed images. Our attention is drawn to the central panel, where a bucket of molten steel, supernatural in its radiance, descends through a partially open window. Intruding from the right is a barrage of fiery red and orange lipsticks, extended combatively. The event at the left is more tranquil, although equally disconcerting: A brown paper bag filled to overflowing with groceries is unexpectedly turned upside down, the contents miraculously remaining inside. Inferences of war, sex, violence, passion, industry, and domesticity may be drawn from these images. The painting can thus be read as a metaphor for the contradictory nature of American society today.

In *House of Fire* Rosenquist's use of commercial techniques and materials, his elimination of visible brushwork, and his hard-edged application of paint, which has grown more glossy and photo-realistic over the years, are typical of his style and serve to characterize Pop Art in general.

Lisa Mintz Messinger

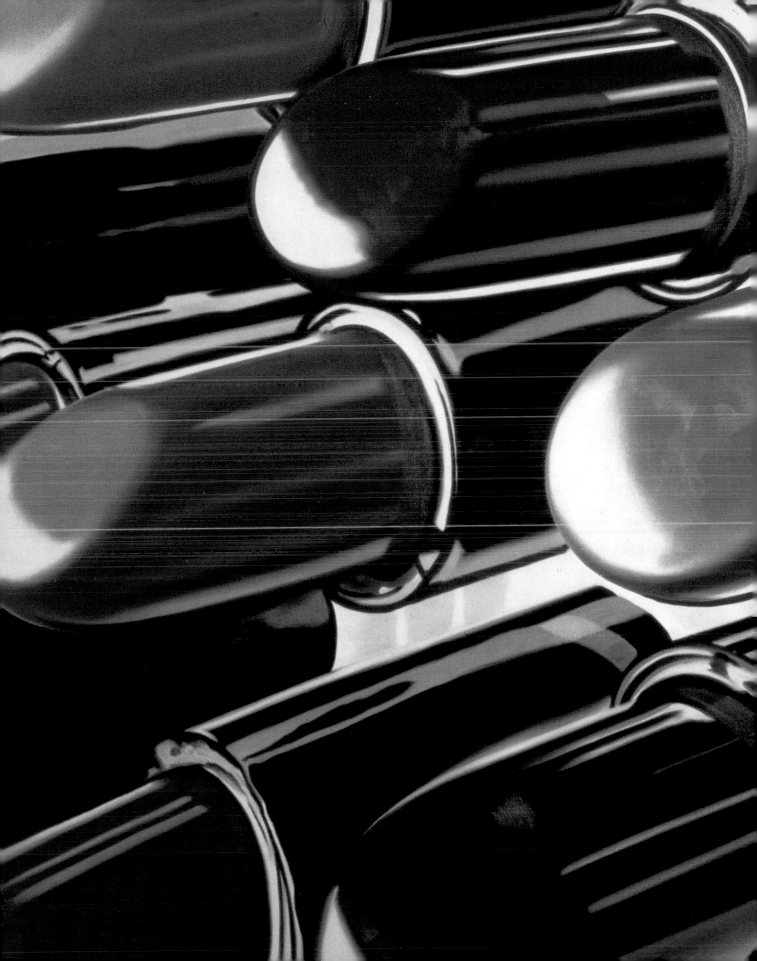

BASELITZ: *Man of Faith*, 1983

Oil on canvas, 97 ½ x 78 in.
Gift of Barbara and Eugene Schwartz, 1985
(1985.450.1)

SINCE 1969 the brutal, expressionist paintings of Georg Baselitz have depicted figures upside down. This device was previously the hallmark of another artist, Marc Chagall, whose people, floating free through time and space, were used to a very different purpose—as elements of a complex narrative. In Baselitz's work the inverted figure focuses our immediate attention not on the narrative subject but on the process of painting itself— on the textural qualities of the oil medium, the vivid contrasts of color, and the violent, agitated brushwork. The shock of seeing reality presented "on its ear" is perhaps too much for the viewer to overlook completely, but we may concede that Baselitz has succeeded in creating a tense balance between representation and abstraction.

In *Man of Faith* Baselitz has produced a simple, disturbing image on a grand scale (the canvas is more than eight feet tall), and he fills almost the entire composition with the form of the falling man. Dressed in what appear to be clerical robes, the figure is bent over in prayer, perhaps a reference to the Apostle Peter, who was crucified upside down. The same man appears with three other figures in a larger horizontal painting done a few months later. The figure's fetuslike body is surrounded by a jagged halo of energized paint, which heightens the sensation of rapid descent and also defines the outline of the body against the similarly colored background. Baselitz's color is dark and powerful—primarily deep blue-blacks, with patches of bright white, yellow, and blue. The coarse style of painting, derived from early 20th-century German Expressionism, is equally stark and direct, and subject and technique together achieve what Baselitz calls "aggressive harmony."

Lisa Mintz Messinger

KITAJ: *John Ford on His Deathbed,* 1983–84

Oil on canvas, 60 x 60 in.
Purchase, Lila Acheson Wallace Gift, 1986
(1986.4)

LIKE DICKENS, Dostoyevsky, and Tolstoy, R. B. Kitaj explores the human character, and he too relies on telling psychological detail. His painting is expressionistic but controlled by intellect rather than fevered by emotion. An American, Kitaj has lived for thirty years in London, where he has been mentor and friend to several younger British artists, among them David Hockney (see page 48), whom he met in 1960 when they were students at the Royal College of Art.

Kitaj has been a prolific printmaker, innovatively exploiting the graphic possibilities of silkscreen. His painting, rather different in style, was influenced first by the technique and texture of his pastels, but recently what he has depicted on canvas—and it is always arresting—is completely painterly in execution and effect. And, in some of his subjects at least, he has returned to the United States.

In 1970 in Hollywood Kitaj visited John Ford, the legendary film director. Their encounter was brief, but it remained pictorially vivid in the painter's mind. Here we see Ford on his deathbed, propped up against the pillows. As he tells the beads of his rosary, the dying man summons up images from his favorite films. At the far left stands the tall Irish Sergeant Mulcahy from *Fort Apache* (1948), complete with his

dress uniform and gloves. The couple dancing around a maypole reminds us that Ford frequently used such scenes to preface grim events, as in *Drums Along the Mohawk* (1939). Ford appears again at the bottom left as he looked during the shooting of *The Quiet Man* (1952). He sits in a director's chair and speaks through a megaphone to two actors, a dissolute and desolate pair from *Tobacco Road* (1941). Above Ford's bed is a framed black-and-white still photograph from the film he most liked, *The Sun Shines Bright* (1954). It shows a prodigal woman of shame returning home to see her daughter before she dies. In another frame appear two words that read "The End."

William S. Lieberman

INDEX